Listening

Thea Holly

www.capallbann.co.uk

Listening To Trees

ISBN 186163 112X

Internal illustrations and photographs by the author
Cover design by Paul Mason

Published by:

Capall Bann Publishing
Freshfields
Chieveley
Berks
RG20 8TF

Dedication

I would like to dedicate my book to my very special family, friends and beloved pets, on both sides of Life, my wonderful Spirit Helpers, Mrs. Kathryn Taylor of the Halifax and of course the Trees and their Guardians.

Contents

Eva and Poppy (Poppy is in the background)

Introduction

I have always loved trees and couldn't imagine living in a world without their presence. I have, for a very long time, felt comfortable with my belief that there exists a parallel stream of evolution that encompasses a hierarchy of beings who attend to the needs of the Natural World. I now know that this commitment extends to the Human Race also.

A few years ago, while walking my dogs Eva and Poppy in the woods above my cottage, I came upon a rough stone that had a quartz-like substance threaded through it. It was beautiful and I stopped and picked it up. I wondered if it would be acceptable for me to take it home and instantly picked up a telepathic communication. I had, since childhood, communicated with spirit friends, relatives and guides of my own and those attached to people that I knew, but this felt different. I was unsure where the communication came from but simply assumed it must be from a human spirit. It never crossed my mind that it might come from the spirits of the trees that surrounded me.

I was told that I could take the stone home but that if ever I left my cottage I would have to put it back where it came from. I agreed to this and took it home. It sits on my doorstep where it soaks up the sun and the rain and if I ever move from this beautiful haven I will, of course return it to the woods.

My love of trees has grown with each passing season and eventually the desire to write about them began to take shape within my mind. I decided that I would investigate the significance placed upon them by different religions throughout history but I found that several books had already been written around this theme. For a while I felt that I had nothing new to offer to the subject but all this was to change when, while out walking with a friend, our dogs running ahead through the mixed woodland of ash, oak, silver birch and other native species, I saw a tree spirit. Let me first explain that as a child I saw as I see all of life but this frightened me. Seeing as I did a nun passing me on the stairs of my childhood home, when I knew that we didn't have any nuns staying with us.

My parents at that time were not able to listen to my tales of sightings with support or understanding and so my fear closed down this ability. In its place there developed what I call my inner screen. It is a difficult concept to explain but I know from experience that there are many people who 'see' as I do and who also communicate telepathically. I am well aware that the notion of trees communicating will never be accepted by the vast majority of people, at least while they remain on this side of life.

I do not claim that trees have a language that only I can receive. I believe that the lessons we can learn from each tree species can be absorbed by anyone willing to open themselves up to the energy of the trees in order to benefit from their ageless wisdom.

Telepathy is a form of communication that is again difficult to explain. Thought has no tangible language, yes, we all think in our native tongue, but something happens when you link in to the energies of a tree. Whatever their form of communication is it takes shape within our minds as words. These words will differ from person to person, but the underlying message will always be the same. Depending upon your level of understanding, the words will suit your ability to receive that message.

After the sighting of the tree spirit I felt that possibly I might find something to contribute to our knowledge of trees. I decided to take a pen and notebook on all my future walks in order to learn more about tree spirits. I had recently come upon a most beautiful sweet chestnut tree in the woodland near my home and decided to make this my first subject. I still marvel at what I was privileged to share with this impressive tree. It opened up a doorway into a realm of support and guidance for me and anyone willing to suspend their disbelief and share in the richness of the wisdom that is available.

At the end of the book I have outlined how you can link in to the energies of a tree to gain healing, guidance and support. You do not have to be psychic in order to benefit from the abundance that is present in Nature, you simply need to be willing to open up your mind to the infinite possibilities that exist all around us.

Sweet Chestnut

The Sweet Chestnut

It was a beautiful sunny morning in July when, with my two black and white springer spaniels, I set out for Bratton Wood. This area of woodland contains many beautiful oak trees, some ash and also holly and a wonderful sweet chestnut tree. The woodland immediately above my cottage contains a mixture of native species and a great number of sycamore which I love.

The National Parks Authority had been clearing large numbers of sycamore and replacing them with oak and ash but I am hopeful that they will continue to retain the older sycamore that grace the slopes of the hills above Woodcombe.

I walked up the familiar track that winds through the woods and on through the little gate that brought me into Bratton Wood. I marvelled at the honeysuckle that wound its way up high into the branches of an oak tree and watched my dogs running through the undergrowth chasing one scent after another.I could see the large sweet chestnut a short distance away and could already see coloured shapes around its base. I sensed both a male and a female presence and gradually was able to see two distinct forms not unlike human figures.

I felt that I should ask permission to step within the tree`s energy field and telepathically received the invitation to do so. My head was full of questions. I mentally asked if the time of day had anything to do with the energy I sensed around the tree.

I was a little confused because by now I had become aware of more beings. To my amazement it was explained to me that I had been expected, that my thoughts regarding the purpose for this walk had been picked up by the other sweet chestnuts trees that I had passed along the track. This was my first lesson. I learned that all trees within one species are linked. The energy or vibration that they emit can be picked up on the air and transmitted from tree to tree as a means of communication. I, too, could somehow link in to this method of communication which I equate with telepathy. As I have said before, I do not believe that trees communicate in words but the energy or vibration that results from a human asking questions of them produces a response that is channelled by the tree spirits who enable us to receive it in the form of words.

I also learned from the sweet chestnut that their message is unique to their specific species and likewise all other trees species have a distinct message for humanity that differs not from tree to tree but from species to species.At last I asked this beautiful old tree about its message for humanity and this was its reply:

"We link in to the mystical questions. We try to settle the doubt and fear and self-denial. We teach of the link to all things, all of life, all of time, now, before and the time to come."

And then to my surprise I was asked a question. "What do you wish to know? We can read your thought patterns but wait for your question to form, to gain permission to answer."I have often wondered about my life's path and freely admit to having found this lifetime not the easiest of passages. This wonderful old tree linked in with my deepest pain and the words took shape inside my head.

"Your life has already had meaning but you have still not accepted your purpose. You feel you are merely a visitor waiting to leave. Of course, you will eventually leave but all of life is waiting for your to surrender to it as we do. Such a

vision will unfold when you let go and accept that you are here to stay. Commit yourself to life itself and it will bear fruit that will enhance your days."

I thanked the tree for its wisdom and turned to walk home. When I looked back I saw the most beautiful colours moving around the base of the tree. Gradually they took shape and I gazed upon three beings who seemed to emit such a wonderful peace that I could have stayed rooted to that spot if it hadn't been for the insistent barking of Eva, who by now was completely fed up of repeatedly placing her ball at my feet for me to throw. I picked up the ball and threw it along the winding path and headed for home. Poppy ran out of a thicket and tried to beat her mother to the ball. Eva picked it up and brought it back for me to throw once more.

As we threaded our way back through Bratton Wood I noticed the many sweet chestnut trees along the way, I hadn't realised how many there were here. Walking again through the little gate that brought me back into the woods above my cottage, I was filled with a new awareness of the energies that surrounded me. They emanated from every tree I passed.

The Ash

The day after my visit to the sweet chestnut in Bratton Wood, I still felt uplifted by the whole experience but have to admit that I had a sneaking feeling that `men in white coats` were waiting round the next tree to take me off to some facility for the deluded.

As far back as I can remember I have conversed happily with Spirit people and they have brought me through some of the most difficult times of my life. They have also given me a great deal of survival evidence for both family and friends. But listening to trees felt very different and although I had seen nature spirits as a child, this development was a little unnerving. However, I shouldn't have been surprised by the sudden extension of my sensing ability.

I have run development circles for the last few years and have come across more and more people who have been completely unaware of the extent of their potential until they were given an opportunity for growth. In some cases their progress has been very rapid.However, the response from some of my friends did make me question the experience. One friend thought it sounded, in her words, 'a little wacky'. This was a bit of a shock since she is a developing medium herself. Another, when I asked her if she thought I was going mad, instead of reassuring me said that at least it sounded like a very pleasant madness.

With my head buzzing around these issues I set out for the woodland above my cottage, once more with my dogs in tow. As before, neither of them appreciated the reason behind my

Looking across to Minehead from Bratton Wood

quest and as usual, after chasing around after one scent or another, Eva brought the ball for me to throw.

By this time I had chosen a large, beautifully shaped ash tree that stands to the left of the path as it winds its ways towards the gate into Bratton Wood. I sent out my request to approach and became aware of a sensitive, feminine energy which I immediately felt comfortable with. The dogs had decided to leave me in peace for the moment in order to investigate the undergrowth beyond this wonderful tree.

I took my opportunity to ask if, like the sweet chestnut, the ash had a message for humanity. Although, I had already been informed, during that first communication, that all tree species carry a message, I still had my doubts as to what I had learned from the sweet chestnut and I suppose I was testing it.

It was a matter of seconds before the words began to spill through my mind and onto my page. *"It is the duty of each soul to seek to live in harmony with itself as we do. Some (people) as you know are not evolved enough to tap the inner depths of their knowledge that link them to all things. We can teach the lesson of harmony, letting go, to live life as you are meant to live it, in trust that Life and all that links us will take care of you."*

I became aware of the ball at my feet and the two dogs poised expectantly for me to throw it. I felt a little irritated by this interruption but, bless them, they had been so patient and I threw it a few times before resuming my link with the tree.*"Look at us,"* the words began to flow again, *"we send up our branches so that our leaves can live in the light. We strive for balance within ourselves, for harmony."*

Then I knew that the spirit of the tree had become aware of my own negative state of mind. I was told to place my hands

Looking across to Bratton Village

on the trunk of the tree and to breathe in deeply and as I exhaled, to let go of my negativity. Then as I breathed in again the negativity would be replaced with the tree's own positive, healing energy. I asked how the tree would replace what I was absorbing and was told that it was all a part of a never ending cycle.I decided to resume my walk and thanked the tree.

Soon the dogs appeared from the undergrowth and once more Eva dropped the ball at my feet. As I threw it back along the path I saw a tree spirit next to the ash, I again sensed a female energy. The features were so gentle but almost bland. The tree spirit seemed to be robed in a garment of brown and cream and as I gazed at this being I was filled with a surge of confidence.

Ash trees are particularly beautiful and I find that I am more at peace within their energy field than with any other species. I think that this is because of its gentle but strong energy which supports my needs at this time. It is hard to put into words what I am able to absorb from the ash trees but is almost like experiencing the most profound nurturing, the kind of nurturing that supports your own inner growth and yet encourages self-responsibility. I hope that gives you some idea of the wonderful energy of these tree.

I decided to retrace my walk along the path and down the track which leads to the lane that runs past my cottage. I had remembered the ash trees that grow beside the stream running parallel to the footpath to Bratton Village. Bratton Village consists of a few white thatched cottages and a wonderful old manor house set in some of the most beautiful countryside in Somerset. I can look across to the village from Bratton Wood which lies almost opposite.

Sometimes in the warm weather I sit in the shade of some old knarled oak trees where the branches almost touch the grass, and look over to the village and marvel at the scene of tranquil beauty. But now I retraced my footsteps past my cottage and on down the lane towards the Bratton footpath. This is a beautiful walk, skirting farmland that is overlooked on both sides by hills.

As the path winds on over the little bridge that crosses the stream you enter a small wooded area and there alongside the footpath are ash trees, oak and some alder.

There is a particularly beautiful ash further along the footpath as it nears Bratton Village. Last year it sadly lost one of its magnificent branches, but it still maintains its dramatic beauty. I stood beneath its great height and mentally sent out my request to step within its aura. I held my pen, poised for any communication and then it began:

"The thread of Life runs through all things. If mankind but knew, understood and accepted this, a respect for all of Nature would result and thus the environment would be protected, nurtured. We do not see this happening and do not sense it for the future, how sad. Mankind`s singular, personal goals often make him blind to the wider implications of his thoughtless actions. He will have to account for all that is done in negativity."

I felt a little let down by this pronouncement for basically I am an optimist and this was not really what I wanted or expected to receive in the way of communication from this lovely tree.I sent out my thanks to the ash and headed for home, the sky had become overcast and the words on my page left me feeling a little low. By the time the dogs and I had reached home, the sky had cleared once more and the sun lit up the hillside above my cottage.

It is some time since those first two experiences with the guardians of the ash trees. I often return to these trees and once again link in with the nature spirits that have evolved as caretakers of these beautiful giants. I often receive personal guidance and always leave feeling again that wonderful sense of having been nurtured.

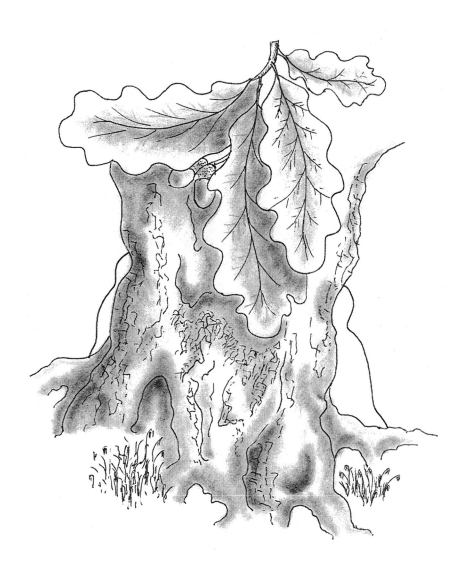

English Oak

The Oak

My next excursion took me back up the lane and onto the path that winds up onto North Hill. Instead of bearing to the left to go on through to Bratton Wood, I continued up the main pathway.

There are a great number of sycamore on either side of the path and on each slope above it. I love them with their graceful branches and their beautiful bark which can glow silvery grey or even a rusty shade of red when the rain has touched it.I walked to the top of the path throwing the ball for the dogs as I went.

My youngest dog, Poppy, has learned that if she is to gain her mother's attention, she must get to the ball first and then off she runs with Eva chasing after her. She eventually drops it and Eva brings it back for me to throw and the whole game starts again. Now and then they discover an interesting scent that interrupts their game and gives me some respite.

On the walk back down the path I was drawn to one of the oak trees that stands close to the path. I have to admit to having already thought about what an oak tree might have to convey but was about to be taught not to have preconceived ideas about this amazing species. Once again, notebook in hand, I sent out my request to approach the tree. I was aware of both male and female energy and the words began to flow.

"We can help the rigid and inflexible to bend a little in order to relax and explore their needs. We can support the timid and frail of heart to become more definite and purposeful."

23

Oak trees at Nutcombe Bottom

This was not what I had expected. I have always associated the oak tree with strength and endurance yet the message I was receiving was that depending upon our needs the oak would supply whatever was necessary for our individual growth and change.I wondered how this change could be brought about and was told that it is by absorbing some of the energy of the tree through breathing while standing within its aura.

Much later I learned that be standing quiet and still, a link would be formed between the energy of the tree and that of the `seeker` and in that way any imbalance or negativity in our energy field could be rectified.I thanked the tree and turned to resume my walk back down the path to my cottage.

But I felt drawn back within its aura and once again the words began to flow.

"You underestimate our teachings, our role within the lives of humans. We can open the door to hidden potential, we can teach you to tap in to all of Life and to link wholly with this Life force to truly enable the human soul to learn to express itself on all levels with confidence. Whatever you wish to be with your whole heart, you can be. We can instill in you the confidence and the courage to achieve great things to fulfil your potential."

I found myself explaining that I didn't underestimate the teachings of this tree species and that I was merely in a hurry to get home after a long walk. I must admit to feeling a little self-conscious, defending myself to a tree and then I became aware of two people approaching with their dogs and decided that it was a good time to resume my walk back down to the cottage.

It is known by some of my neighbours that I run development circles and that, together with a friend, who is also an

The old oak tree hanging horizontally over the dried up river bed at Brockwell

aromatherapist, I work with animals using aromatherapy and spiritual healing but I wasn't ready for word to get about that I also listen to trees.

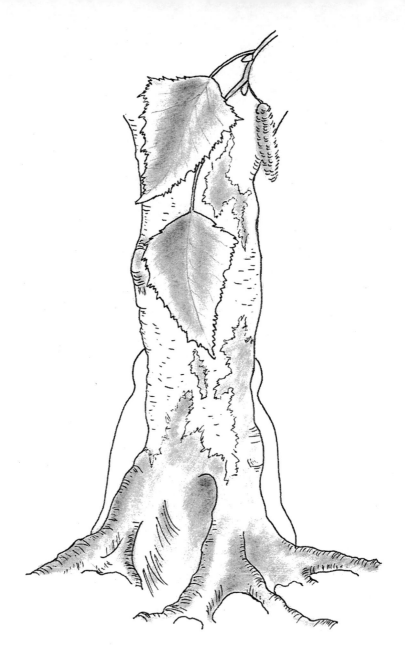

Silver Birch

Silver Birch

The woodland path above my cottage winds its way up to North Hill but it ends in quite a steep climb so now and then I put the dogs into the car and drive up. North Hill is a magical place. On one side you can look out over the estuary to the Welsh Coast, the other overlooks a patchwork of fields and upwards to the moorland of Dunkery Beacon. At the very end of the road you can park your car and let you eyes take in the distant cottages of Porlock and watch the sun set beyond the Lynmouth headland. I have walked here for the past twelve years and never tire of the wonderful views and often find pathways that are new to me.

On this particular morning I wanted to walk among the many silver birch that grow to the right of the first brow of the hill. The majority of these trees are relatively young and it was not until much later in my quest for the wisdom of trees that I came upon silver birch of a much greater age, twisted and roughened by the elements so that unless you could recognise them by their delicate network of branches, they would go unknown during the winter months.

However, these young trees were graceful and their bark was silvery white. I approached with pen and note-book ready and once more the words began to flow. I learned that the silver birch teaches us to be at peace with ourselves, to take one day at a time helping us to achieve inner serenity. The energy of this tree supports those of us who find it hard to release ourselves from emotional trauma and helps us to create a sacred place within, a soul space where we can just be.

Looking across to Dunkery Beacon from North Hill (Dunkery is the highest point on Exmoor).

Looking out over Porlock Bay from Bassington Hill, Lynmouth headland in the distance.

Looking across Porlock Vale towards Bassington Hill.

"We can teach calmness and inner peace and enable the lost to learn to walk and count each step and not to look beyond, to make the best use of each second as an opportunity for growth, inner growth. We teach compassion to the self-obsessed, those who find it so difficult to reach out to another soul. We promote trust in the Human species, courage to reach out, courage to share the same ground, the same space in compassion."

Recently during one of the tree workshops that I run where I endeavour to encourage participants to sense the energies of different species, I had confirmation of the unique healing quality of silver birch energy. I observed one of the group standing within the aura of a particularly old tree. I asked her how she was getting on and she looked at me doubtfully. She had very little confidence in her ability to sense any energies at all. "I'm not sure that I'm sensing anything, except for a pressure around my heart and I do feel a little tearful."

Knowing a little of this dear woman's history I knew that this wonderful old tree had touched her on a deep level and explained what I had previously learned. Her face lit up with such a wonderful smile and for the rest of the day she proceeded with far more confidence than I thought she was capable of.

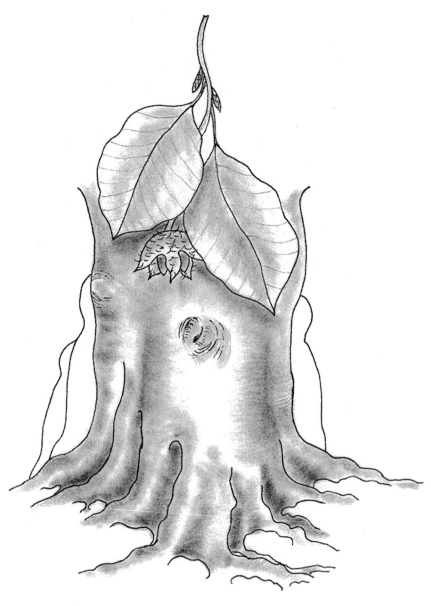

Beech

The Beech

Brockwell is a tiny hamlet you might miss if you didn't know that it was there. It lies below the moorland rise of Robin How. There are only a very few homes there and a sharp bend in the lane where a narrow track can be seen rising up and disappearing into the woodland above. It was here that a friend brought me to see some beautiful beech trees. There is an old enclosed paddock bordered entirely by these wonderful trees. Their shapes twisting and turning and casting strange shadows onto the woodland floor in the warm afternoon light.

An old oak tree has grown at right angles, suspended above a long since dried up river bed and another stands as a sentinel at the head of the gorge.

But I had come to try to link in to the energies of the beech. These trees had always held a special place in my heart, with their serene beauty and air of peace and tranquillity. Yet when I approached and linked in to their energy I felt a negativity directed towards me. I was surprised and felt a little uncertain, I had not expected this. Then the words began to form within my mind.

"We can teach you to look at your life with honesty and clarity, only when you are ready to take stock of where you are and where you should be. We can help you to detach yourself from man's obsession with time and fear of trusting in something greater. Ours is a strong energy and you need courage to work with it as we show you where you are and your true path ahead. Sometimes this takes courage as you cannot hide from yourself."

Brockwell

Beech trees at Webber's Post.

I knew then why I had felt so uncomfortable. I knew that I needed to take stock of my life and to find the courage to commit to a path that I was only tentatively walking. I was afraid of placing my whole trust in an uncertain future and yet I had such support and encouragement from my Spirit Teachers, why was it so hard to let go and trust?

I walked away from the tree feeling a strange sense of rejection but now looking back I know that this wonderful tree was merely holding up a mirror for me but I wasn't ready to gaze at the reflection.

In the last few months I have plunged myself more deeply into working with Spirit and now run more courses and workshops in order to pass on what I am learning from my Spirit Helpers.

During the first tree workshop that I ran up in Selworthy woods, again I came upon a beautiful beech tree whose leaves where just beginning to unfurl in the first warmth of Spring. I had deliberately avoided working with beech trees since that upsetting experience at Brockwell but as workshop leader I had to be available for the participants in order to encourage them to link in with the energies of each of the different tree species.

I could see, as I observed different members of the group working with some of the trees, that one of the group, together with her young daughter, had settled under the large beech tree that grew on the other side of the stream. I felt a little apprehensive as I approached the tree to see how they were getting on but I instantly felt a welcome from the tree and absorbed the words "'You are here." I was then shown myself standing between darkness and light and knew that the tree had sensed that I had moved on in my life. I felt uplifted by the whole experience.

Douglas Fir

Selworthy is a lovely old unspoiled village made up of cream coloured thatched cottages set in some of the most beautiful countryside in West Somerset. It is part of the Holnicote Estate bequeathed by Lord Acland to the National Trust.

Part of the charm of this lovely area is the old white-washed church with its wonderful view of the valley fields below and the brooding moorland rising up in the distance. There is a pathway beside the church that runs along the stream and as you follow the track you pass ancient silver birch, so old and altered from their silvery white youth that only the leaves in the Spring or the fine filigree of delicate branches in Winter give a clue to their species.

Following the path as it climbs upwards you also pass sycamore, beech, oak, ash, rowan, holly and a lone holm oak with its dark green leathery leaves which it keeps all year long, and its strange bark, like elephant hide. It stands, towering over the path as it offers you a choice of directions, left and upwards to some delicate larches, pine and douglas fir or right to the magnificent wellingtonia just below Lady Acland`s memorial hut.

I planned to work with the energy of the douglas fir. A wonderful specimen stands almost at the top of the path, its main branch hanging over the track, its enormous weight threatening to bring the tree crashing down around you. A short distance beyond this is another one, instead of growing tall and straight, the exposed position has invited strong winds to control the growth of this remarkable tree. It is quite short and its limbs grow curled and yet it has a dramatic

Douglas Fir

beauty which draws me. The day was cold and the wind cut through me, my dogs were insistent and every now and then I had to stop my attempts to link in with the tree, to throw the ball. Eventually, they took pity on me and ran off to investigate a bramble patch. I found the energy of this species challenging, a little like that of the beech but if anything a little gentler.

It was explained to me that in order to make the best use of the energy of this species, you need to clear your mind of any negativity, to let go of past problems, emotional trauma. The energy of this tree works best for those people wishing to completely change their lives. It helps you to tap in to your inner courage in order to implement the necessary changes to promote a new direction in life, one of spiritual growth. Again, as with the beech, I am sure that I found this energy challenging simply because I had, not yet reached my own necessary crossroads. The signs were all there but at that time I lacked the courage to read the message.

After a while I began to sense the presence of the tree guardian and saw a being in white. I felt that I was being observed with tolerance and patience. If this gentle being could feel tolerant and patient towards me perhaps I should also be a little gentler towards myself.

I thanked the guardian of the tree and turned back to walk down the track, to dogs came spilling out of the undergrowth and caught up with me. Eva dropped the ball at my feet. I threw it ahead of us down the sloping path. Away from the exposed hilltop the wind no longer cut through me. The light was beginning to fade but now and then the last rays of the sun caught the rise and fall of the stream as the water tumbled over the stones on its journey downwards.

The main path up through Selworthy woodland.

Holm Oak

After working with the energy of the douglas fir, although the light was beginning to fade I felt drawn towards a holm oak that stood with a small number of others up on the slope above the stream. I had passed it on my way up the path and it had looked quite sombre as it cast its shadow over the fallen limbs of another once great tree.

I mentally asked for permission to approach and sensed a comforting energy. I leaned my back against the trunk of this wonderful tree and closed my eyes. Images began to flood onto my inner screen and I could see that I was encircled by a group of beings in white. All were hooded but one, who held out a circular bowl to me that seemed to contain water.

I was told to splash the water on my head and face. I visualized myself doing this and felt refreshed. The circle of beings seemed to be bathed in a bright light. I was told that my energy was not balanced and to breathe in deeply to absorb healing energy from the tree.I mentally asked for the message of the Holm Oak and was told that, as with the English Oak, it was a message of balance.

The Oak species give to us what we need, whether it is guidance in order to let our life flow a little more, or a gentle discipline in order to see a clearer way forward.Since this first encounter with the energy of this species I have come upon a most wonderful woodland where almost every tree is a holm oak.

Beneath Selworthy Beacon, at the end of North Hill there are paths down to the left that eventually lead to the villages of

Holm Oak

Allerford and Bossington, both unspoiled jewels in Somerset's crown. The paths wind this way and that, and one leads you downward through an avenue of holm oak. The slopes either side of the path are all graced by these beautiful trees and the energy from this magical place is truly unique. When I first came upon this haven I had to simply stand in quiet reverence of the tangible peace and sanctity that fills the air.I felt that I was being nurtured within a dark yet sacred womb.I felt a connection with Mother Earth like nothing I had felt before. I felt safe, I felt loved. I return again and again to this peaceful oasis to soak up the beauty of it all.

Rowan

The Rowan

A few days after my visit to the woodland above Selworthy, I returned to wander again among the few holm oaks, rowan and silver birch that dot the hillside above the stream.

Although the air was still a little crisp, the sun was warm on my face as I stood with my eyes closed, drawing in its wonderful energy. I retraced my footsteps through the holm oaks to a glade of silver birch on the crest of the hill and there one tree stood out from all the rest. It looked as if the top had been sheared off by lightning and all the lower branches were devoid of leaf buds. In their place hung what local people call witches brooms that look more like birds` nests. There were tiny leaflets growing out of balls of twigs, suspended from the branches like hanging baskets.

But what really delighted me were the wood anemones growing in a cradle of moss within the trunk of this magical tree.

I walked back along the track to sit down beside a large rowan. The ground was a little damp but I didn't mind, I had been drawn to this tree as I passed it earlier and just felt I had to return and sit within its aura. The bark had an almost grey metallic look to it and the delicate white florets were beginning to show their petals.

I felt myself relax into the energy emanating from this tree and took up my pen and note-book. The energy was light and I sensed a feminine presence. After a while I could see a form taking shape a little distance from the tree. Soft yellows swirled about as the form developed. The face that looked back at me expressed such gentle warmth and support and once more words started to fill my page as I tried to write down all that was being conveyed to me.

"We enable people to be lighter in spirit. We work well with those who take themselves and their problems too seriously. Linking in with our energy can help you to put all this into perspective, lifting your vibrations. We can help you to raise your awareness in order to link in more easily to the energy of other tree species that may at first seem a little difficult to sense."

The tree guardian moved closer and I felt her eyes look deep within mine, to the core of my being. I felt myself absorb a gentle warmth from this being and then it was gone.

The mood had been broken, my attention diverted as Eva placed a stick in my lap. Poppy had the ball and Eva had given up trying to get it back. They had almost been invisible to me until that moment. I had been lost, suspended in a warm glow. I stood up and thanked the tree and made my way down the slope back onto the main path.

I suddenly felt a little cold, it was strange. Time had seemed to stand still there beneath that rowan, I had felt safe and content and would have stayed there indefinitely but for Eva and her stick.

The Alder

Some time ago during the winter, I had walked the little footpath to Bratton village to try to link in with the energy of the alder trees that grow in profusion there. They love the water and are dotted here and there along the edge of the stream.

At that time I had experienced difficulty linking in to the energy of these trees and so a while ago I returned to try again. Young ones have also been planted the other side of the footpath and stand there holding on to their cones while also displaying their catkins. In the field that borders the footpath there was a herd of Friesian cows. They seemed to me to be as curious as cats for they began to keep pace with the dogs as we wandered along the path. When I stopped to look at a tree, the dogs stopped and the group of cows, whose interest we had captured, stopped also. Eventually they lost interest and continued to graze, only occasionally raising their heads to check on our progress. I chose an alder to work with and sensed such a gentle, light energy and began to pick up the message that was being transmitted.

"When you are ready to strive for a spiritual way forward through your life, we teach you to let go. You find us by running water, listen to it, give up your knotted fear of living a different life. Those of you who set yourselves free from a life that does not allow spiritual expression, will be nurtured once you learn to tap in to the Life force that lies within all things. Even the air is not seen and understood for what it can bring you. Its energy changes throughout the day. Sit quietly and absorb it at different times during the day and study its

49

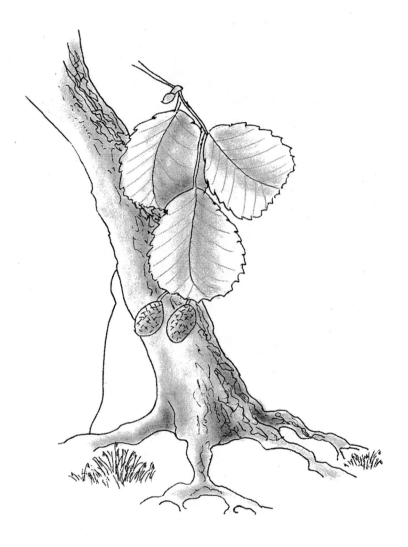

Alder

healing qualities for yourself."

As with other tree species I felt I was being observed by the guardian of this tree. I sensed amusement at my notetaking and became aware of a feminine presence swathed in vibrant coloured light, yellow, orange, green, changing. I thanked the alder and resumed my walk along the footpath to Bratton.

Further along this path are two trees that I always visit when I take this route. The first is the great ash that towers above the path. At present there are still a few violets growing around its base. Ever since I first worked with the energy of that first ash tree that stands by the woodland path above my cottage, I had often sought out the energy of these trees in order to link in and seek personal guidance. I have struggled for a long time to commit myself completely to trusting the guidance I get from Spirit Helpers and also from the trees themselves as regards my material life.

Although I am being presented with more and more opportunities to work as a medium and teacher within the field of spiritual and psychic development, I still find it difficult to let go of more conventional means of keeping the roof above my head. And yet time and time again, when I approach the ash for guidance the same message is repeated. "Let go of the past and trust that you will be taken care of." I have been through many dark tunnels in my time and have allowed myself to almost expect another one just around the corner. But the wisdom of the trees speaks deeply to me and I am getting closer and closer to the point of letting go.

The second tree along this footpath is a huge oak that overlooks the stream. It has a wonderful aura of strength and conviction. I never pass by without asking to simply lean my back against its trunk and then it`s as if the world stands still and I feel held in an energy field from which I can absorb what I need to strengthen me in my purpose.

Scots Pine

The Scot Pine

Dunster lies a few miles from my home and I often walk in the woodland that covers the knoll overlooking the edge of the town. There is a folly right at the top of the hill and although the woodland is not large in expanse, I have managed to get lost at least twice in my attempts to find it.

The woodland here is home to some of the largest sweet chestnuts I have seen. There are also many other species such as oak, beech, ash, holly, maple and pine. Where the first track leaves the main path, a huge oak stands watching over those who come and go. Walking along the second track, having climbed up the steep main path, you find yourself looking down through mixed woodland and across to the estuary. Sometimes you can see the steam train on its route to and from Bishops Lydeard and glancing further to the left you can see the proud headland rising up above Minehead.

The dogs love it up here and Poppy often disappears into the trees chasing different scents but always checking to make sure that I'm still somewhere in view. Eva, however, rarely rushes off, she would rather stay with me and chase after the ball. Now and then I must admit that I make wild gestures of throwing it and then quickly pocket it, she will then spend ages looking for it, giving me time to work with the tree energies.

On our first excursion into the woodland, following the path as it curved around to the left and then right into a little clearing, we came upon the ruins of a wall and there some distance in front of it stands an enormous lone scots pine. There are many pine trees in the area, on the slopes of the

Minehead, a view from behind Dunster Knoll

knoll, upon North Hill, at the entrance to Dunster Castle, but this one is truly magnificent. It stands tall and straight, its branches extending from its huge trunk in a wonderful symmetrical pattern.You can stand and look up through its canopy at the sky and get a sense of how small you really are.

The first sight of this tree almost took my breath away. I leaned my back against the pine and stood quietly linking into the energies around me. Again I felt that I was being observed. I sensed a benign, masculine energy and then became aware of the presence of two other beings near by, watching. I felt accepted here and soon the words began to form.

"We can teach Humankind to link in with its own species at the deepest level of recognition. We can stimulate your inner resources and illuminate the inner flame, encouraging it to grow. We can help you to recognise those of your species who are on a similar path and enable you to clarify your vision of that pathway. We can encourage you to be steadfast in your purpose."

I asked what was meant by "the inner flame". I believed it to be a reference to the spark of life within all things. This was acceptable to the guardian of the tree. It was then explained to me that the energy of this species is quite simple to access and I was told that my own energy levels were depleted, I had spent the last two days teaching at a school an hour and a half away from my home. The daily journey always took a lot out of me. I was still recovering from major surgery several months earlier and my energy levels were easily drained. So once more I leaned into the trunk of the tree and this time breathed in deeply and tried to imagine that as I breathed out, I was releasing all my fatigue. I left the little clearing feeling uplifted and revived.

Yew

The Yew

I had learned of the great age of some of the yew trees in the area and wanted to try to work with this ancient wisdom. I didn't expect to find any up on Dunster knoll but one of the paths leads you right between two of them that stand either side of the track. They do not appear to be as old as the ones in Selworthy churchyard and certainly not anywhere near the age of the one at Ashbrittle, reputed to be over three thousand years old. But they have an air of mystery all their own and I was surprised and delighted to come upon them.

When I was a child of about seven I would walk along a pathway to school that bordered a field of cows. I have always loved cows and had a name for each member of the herd. I also knew how curious they could be and would deliberately drag my school bag along the path behind me because I had discovered that by doing so I could guarantee company, the other side of the fence, all the way to the end of the field. One early winter evening a lorry could be seen by the gate and two dead cows were dragged out of the field, their stomachs bloated. My mother explained to me that they must have eaten some yew berries, for yew trees grew at the field`s edge. I felt a deep hatred for yew trees for quite some time after that.

All this had eased and as I approached one of the yew trees I felt a tangible calm descend upon me. I gradually became aware of a being in white, I sensed a female energy and held my pen ready to record whatever came.

Looking towards Minehead headland from Dunster Knoll

"We touch the deepest recesses of your soul, we can encourage you to link deeper and higher than you think is possible. We enable you to link within your soul group, to recognise the connections, if you were to link in with sincerity and honesty we can help you to uncover your past lives and enable you to see destiny`s path running through each one. Be not afraid of this, it brings enlightenment to one`s purpose."

I felt in awe of these words but although I have had glimpses of past lives I was not ready to try to trace the thread back in a more deliberate way. I hope that one day I feel strong or brave or centred enough to work with this wonderful wisdom.

The dogs and I threaded our way further along the track and soon it began to descend and we once more found ourselves on the main path. I was now aware of the sound of rushing traffic on the A39 and I realised that I had been quite unaware of it until that moment, lost in the peace and tranquillity of that timeless woodland.

Sycamore

Sycamore

Sycamore grow in profusion up on the slopes above the cottage. There are also oak, ash, hawthorn, a few beech and some holly too, but the vast majority of trees are sycamore. They grow easily and often create the most beautiful shapes with their limbs arcing up to the light above. With so many, their leaves provide a huge canopy of cool green during the summer months.

I love the smooth texture of the bark when the trees are young and the dramatic shapes created when the bark begins to crack and flake when they are old and well established. Sometimes the colour of the bark resembles soft grey almost with the sheen of silk and yet when the rain touches the bark there can be traces of coppery red. It is a truly beautiful tree with leaves to match its grace.

One summer I was distressed to find a carpet of young sycamore leaves covering the woodland floor when I took my dogs up into the woods above the cottage. I had been walking new paths above Porlock and was quite stunned to see so many leaves under the trees. I realised that this was as a result of quite a long dry spell but quickly received communication from the trees around me. I was told not to upset myself because they had shed their leaves in order to protect the main body of the trees due to the shortage of water. I felt a kind of gentle, understanding energy emanate from these sycamores, rather like a mother explaining away a problem to a worried child.

I love the energy of the sycamore. It is sensitive, yet strong. When I linked in to gain an understanding of their wisdom I learned that they work well with people who have a particularly emotional nature.

"We can encourage greater stability in order to help the oversensitive of your species make sense of their world. Sometimes it is hard for those delicate souls to function in the material world in such a way as to protect themselves from those who are less sensitive.

Learning to link in and absorb our healing energy can help these souls tap an inner strength that can help them to function without absorbing too much hurt. We can enable them to retain their sensitivity and yet create a stronger core in order to survive your sometimes harsh world. We have a deep sympathy for these sensitive souls and can encourage them to take a step forward on their individual path without relinquishing their special gift of sensitivity."

I was aware of a very balanced energy emanating from these trees, sensitive but strong and supportive. I could see swirls of soft green and pale yellow forming around the trunk of the nearest tree and soon I could pick out gentle features looking back at me.

Here in this woodland, ash grow comfortably alongside the sycamore, sometimes seeming to grow out of the same spot, limbs entwined together. Some time ago I stood between an ash and a sycamore, one hand upon either trunk, linking in to their energies. I felt the energies meet down the mid-line of my whole body, half of me experienced the strong, supportive and uplifting energy of the ash, the other half absorbed the sensitive and nurturing of the sycamore. The two energies have similarities and yet the subtle differences can be felt when you have the opportunity to link in with both trees at the same time. With the energy of the beech and the douglas fir, I felt challenged to change, to move forward. The energy of the ash I find nurturing, strong and supportive without being specifically challenging and yet I have gained a lot of personal guidance from linking in with the guardians of these trees. The sycamore seems to me to accept exactly where and who you are, I don`t feel a challenging energy and yet it is clear to me that there are great possibilities for personal growth if you work with this particular species.

A couple of years ago the National Parks Authority, who oversee the care of parts of the hills above the cottage, began to clear-fell quite a large area of sycamore. They planted oak and ash where they had felled these beautiful trees. I telephoned their local office expressing my concern and distress and it was explained that there was a policy to remove certain areas of sycamore and replace them with native species. Sycamore was introduced to Britain, from France, in the Middle Ages. I would have hoped that by now it could be viewed as almost a native species. Sweet Chestnut is also another species that did not originate in Britain - I only hope that there are no plans to rid the woodlands of Britain of this fine species too. The National Parks Authority stopped their felling after a few weeks and the following spring the area was covered with the mauve glow from hundreds of foxgloves. There are still a large number of sycamore up in the woods and many of the larger ones were left untouched but I felt very sad at the felling of so many beautiful trees.'

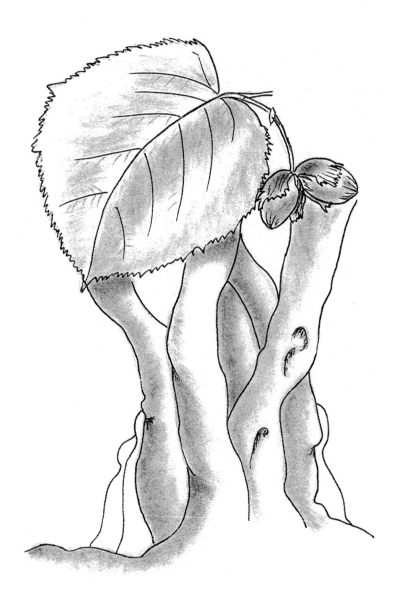

Hazel

The Hazel

Taking the Luccombe turning off the Porlock road and following signs for Cloutsham, you find yourself in the narrow country lanes that are typical of this part of West Somerset. As you rise up towards Webbers Post, you pass through beech woodland, which share the slopes either side of the lane, with ash, oak and holly. The lane rises steeply and then you have a choice, to continue on up the incline to Exmoor`s highest point, Dunkery Beacon, or to branch off right past Webbers Post and on down into the valley to Cloutsham.

The lane that takes you into the valley is very narrow with a few passing places. Either side of it oak trees cling precariously to the steep slopes. Now and then if you dare to look downwards through the trees you may catch a glimpse of the stream below you. Once the lane begins to level out you pass over the ford and driving a little further, the stream now to your left, you come to a place where you can safely park. Here, there is a small open secluded field, bordered on one side by the stream, and then by ash trees set into a stone wall and grassy bank.

I occasionally bring the dogs here, they love to tumble in and out of the water, chasing shadows. I love the peace of this ancient woodland and it is here that I came upon a very old hazel tree. Actually, it is really several growing together, their limbs intertwined. Each trunk of these old trees must be at least a metre in circumference. It grows in the centre of the small, open field, hanging over a bank. It has a lovely light, uplifting energy and linking in with it I sensed the presence of the trees` guardian. I began to ask the role of this guardian

The stream at Cloutsham

The stream at Cloutsham (further up)

and got the reply that it was one of many. I sensed a male energy but became aware that there was also a female energy present. I was eventually able to see a seemingly young figure, quite human in features, swathed in greens and browns. I could not see a figure linked to the female energy. I am aware that the vibrations given off by the guardians of the trees form figures that my mind can accept. In the same way the energy that the tree spirits channel from the trees, form words that I can understand at my present level of development.

I was told that the energy of this tree species can help where people are faced with a number of choices, where there is a sense that they have arrived at a cross-roads in their life.

"We can help you to clarify your needs to enable you to more easily identify your priorities. It takes inner strength to place your needs first, but how can you reach out to others if you are in the darkness yourself."

I could feel the energy of the hazel working on my heart centre and became aware of an inner voice telling me that I needed more laughter in my life. Then again the guardian was telling me that it was one among many. I asked what its role was with this tree and the reply came back.

"Just as you have Spirit Helpers to help guide you forward and to help you to make the best use of your life, so we are here for the benefit of the tree in all things and also to create a bridge between the Natural World and that of the Human Species."

I am well aware that information that I receive is restricted to my level of development and so although I had many more questions I did not ask them, for I felt that at this time I may not be evolved enough to understand the answers. However, another reason for me not continuing with my questions revolved around Eva, who was repeatedly placing the ball between my feet as I endeavoured to link in with the energy of the hazel. Now and then, Poppy would seize her chance to grab at the ball and send me off-balance in more ways than one. I sensed amusement from the tree spirit and said my thank yous and walked back towards the car. I looked again at the beautiful ash trees that had grown tall above the stone and grassy bank. Nestled in the cleft of one of the trees grew a clump of wood sorrel and growing out of the moss below were some violets, all growing together in harmony.

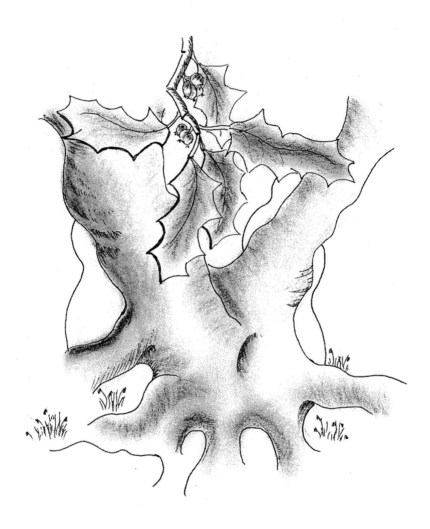

Holly

The Holly

Until I moved to the West Country I was unaware that the holly could grow to quite a substantial height, sometimes reaching over twenty metres. I had only seen bushes or spindly trees that on the rare occasion, some householder had allowed to grow in their garden.

On most of the paths that I have walked, since I came to this beautiful haven, I have come across holly that not only grows tall and strong but expresses its beauty in the most graceful curves of its trunk and branches.

If you care to look in most tree guide books, the bark of the holly is usually described as grey. This does not do justice to the almost metallic silk-like sheen or to the delicate pink shades that sometimes intermingle with the soft grey. It is a wonderful tree, giving us shade from the sun and the rain. It offers us the glory of its dark green leaves all the year round and its startling red berries with which we often decorate our homes at Christmas. Yet it is probably only when this festive season draws near that most of us even take a second look at this lovely tree.

When I decided to go out into the woods to work with the energy of this tree, I chose to walk in Bratton wood. There are many holly trees here but I had noticed one in particular a short distance from that magnificent old sweet chestnut that had first opened up my mind to all the wisdom and guidance that exists around me.

During the first tree workshop that I ran, at the end of the day we all gathered in Selworthy Tea-room for a well deserved hot drink and piece of cake. The day had been cold but not a single drop of rain had fallen and the sun had at last made an appearance during the afternoon. We chatted about the day and I finally asked the group if any of them had felt a negative energy from any of the trees.

One of the group said that she had and I asked her if she would mind answering a personal question. The group had got on so well together and it seemed that an atmosphere of trust had grown between us all and so I was told that I could ask my question. I asked if there was something negative in her life that she was not tackling because the fear of making a change was too great. She agreed that this was the case and then I repeated what I had learned from the holly. The message is basically to let go of negativity, face your fear and make your changes. Her face lit up and she felt that now she could go and work with energy of the holly, knowing that the negativity she had felt was merely being mirrored back at her to show her where she was at that time in her life.

The holly had communicated a great deal more than this to me during my walk in Bratton wood all those months before.

"I was here yesterday, I am here today and I will be here tomorrow. My message is of Life`s continuum. When I finally fall, my seed will already be rising up around me. Does this tell you something?"

I had tentatively replied - "Life goes on?".

The message being communicated through the guardian of this lovely holly continued.

"Yes. Let go of sorrow, let go of negativity and fear. Link with the spirits of the trees, absorb their healing vibrations. Link in

and see the colours, they can enhance your life. Colour has its own healing magic. My message and that of my species is to let go of the negativity that holds you back. This is hard for many of your kind, effort is needed to achieve this letting go, but once achieved, even momentarily, a way forward can be shown to you. It is all about trusting. Under difficult circumstances it may seem impossible to do but again we say, effort is needed. Look back over your life and see where you have come from. The road is long but you are not alone."

I was then instructed to breathe in deeply and visualise any negativity being exhaled. I thanked the tree and the tree guardian and walking back through the wood I realised that although I hadn't thought I was feeling a little low before I approached the holly, I now felt so much lighter that I knew that something had been lifted away from me.

Blackthorn

The Blackthorn

I was walking in the woods above the cottage a few months later when suddenly Poppy and Eva shot off through some young ash trees, obviously after yet another interesting scent. But then I heard squeals and chasing after them I saw a pig disappearing through the hedge into the smallholding to the right of the track.

I had previously seen areas of exposed soil as if some creature had been digging for roots but thought it had been the work of badgers. I knew that the farrier and his partner, who live in one of the cottages, kept pigs on their smallholding and so after the sighting I knew it must be the work of the pig.

I saw her again on a number of occasions, she was quite shy, and would take off just at the sight of me. Probably the memory of the chase was still a bit too fresh in her mind. Her name is Fiona and she is quite a character. Although, the enclosure has since been strengthened I did notice new areas of exposed soil once again the other morning. Fiona is being kept as a breeding sow and so I take comfort in the fact that this delightful pig will live out her days in her idyllic home.

It was after one of my sightings of Fiona that I decided to try to link in with the energy of the blackthorn. It grows in profusion up in the woodland above the cottage and in particular along the edge of the track. In some places it grows in straggly clumps but there is a little blackthorn tree, beautifully proportioned that has found a home close to one of the oak trees that stands by the side of the path.

I thought that I might find it difficult to distinguish its energy from that of the oak because it stands within the aura of this great tree. But the vibrations were different. There was a perfect balance of male and female energy and soon I was able to absorb the message of this species.

I was told that the energy works well for people who have suffered the loss of a child or the pain of infertility. It helps us to rise above the obsession in some, of motherhood, in order to free us to embrace the role of mother to all of life. It helps us to be able to function as a giver and also a receiver. It encourages us to receive compassion from the energies of the Natural World which can shift emotional blocks that hamper our progress.

I was told, not unkindly, that some use bereavement almost as a crutch, to enable them to avoid moving forward. This energy helps us to see that moving forward need not be a frightening choice. I felt comfortable with the energy of this little tree and also felt an almost benevolent vibration emanating from the oak which encircled the blackthorn.

I called the dogs, they had raced off in the direction of the stream to retrieve the ball that one of them had dropped earlier. Then we made our way back down the track, I had hoped to catch another glimpse of Fiona but she was keeping well out of our way.

The Elδer

Sharing the woodland above the cottages are the often twisted trunks and boughs of the elder trees. In winter they look as if the life within has vacated them completely, leaving them dried up and lifeless. And yet come the spring, green shoots begin to burst forth, heralding the delicate elderflowers and then in the autumn, the ripening berries offer fruit not only to the birds but also to any enterprising wine or preserve maker.

There is a short path that runs parallel to the main track, half hidden by brambles, blackthorn and nettles. It is here that an old knarled elder tree stretches its trunk across this little track. Part of the trunk lies along the ground before rising and arching over your head. It is to this tree that I came to seek the wisdom of this old species.

I felt a little tired and so it took some time for me to link into its energy and then the words began to form.

"I am as old as time itself, for I can tap into all of time. We endeavour to do the best with what we have, no matter how mis-shapen we become and so we can encourage your species to tap into their inner depths and develop what is there so that you can achieve your highest goal."

The tree encouraged me to stop looking back into my past and to release myself from the negative conditioning that I have been working hard to reject. Sometimes with the best intentions a mother coping with her own emotional pain can effect the inner confidence of her child.

Elder

I sensed an ancient energy that carried a maternal and strong nurturing element. I was told that I was about to begin the rest of my life's journey with a more confident vision, that I would succeed in letting go of the shadows of the past and at last begin to enjoy the rays of the sun.

I learned that the elder can encourage us to emerse ourselves in all that is good, to be creative, to put out our hand to another soul, to accept the pain that we go through as an apprenticeship for the service of others, in order to shine our light out into the darkness. I have known since childhood that none of us are ever alone. We are all surrounded by spirit helpers, who endeavour to make themselves known to us in order to guide us and support us. But I was learning that these wonderful trees also have a role to play on our pathway through life.

I gradually became aware of a sound breaking into my link with this lovely old tree. It wasn't the dogs, it was a sort of loud snuffling sound. I thanked the tree and called the dogs to me as I suddenly remembered what the sound was. There was a pig loose and I didn't want Eva and Poppy traumatising Fiona again. I put the leads on the dogs and headed back onto the main track where the snuffling sound grew louder and then I saw them. Fiona had brought her friend Hamish on her afternoon adventure, and together they were investigating the undergrowth above the stream. Hamish, like Fiona, is a sow but her owners had run out of female Scottish names and chose this unusual alternative, but it seems to suit her. Neither of them were the least bit concerned to see the dogs or myself and after looking up to see who was coming down the track, they lowered their heads and continued munching.

The sightings of my neighbour's pigs took place in the Spring of 1999 and after that final escape the fencing was secured successfully.

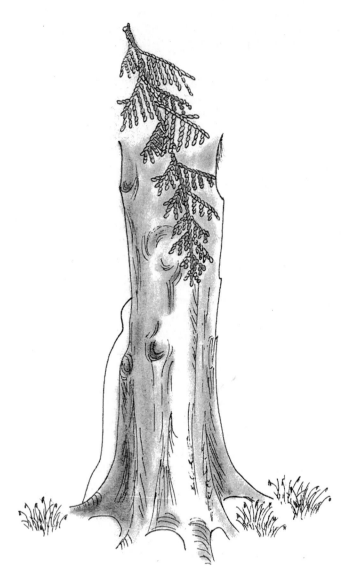

Cypress

Cypress (Lawson)

Soon after the encounter with Hamish and Fiona, I decided to investigate the woodland the other side of Dunster. A short distance after turning into the lane that takes you up over Croydon Hill and on to Luxborough, there is a mixed woodland of broadleaved trees and forestry owned by the Crown Estate. This is Nutcombe Bottom and it is open to the public. I had never walked here before but had often passed the entrance on my way to Luxborough.

The dogs were so excited, they love the adventure of walking anywhere but somewhere that is new presents them with a special pleasure and once out of the car, they tore off ahead of me. However, after only a short while they raced back having forgotten to collect their ball from me. As I walked up the steep, curving path, I noticed the tremendous height of some of the oaks by the side of the track. I also passed sweet chestnut, cypress, pines, more oak and douglas fir.

As the path neared the brow of the hill, I noticed five large oak trees that stand in a circle to the left of the track. Even before I approached them I could see that the energy around them was charged. I knew that I had to go and stand within the centre of that circle. I stood there with my eyes closed absorbing the powerful energy from these great trees. I felt after awhile that I was connected to all that was above and below the ground and had a strange sensation of growth. I had to open my eyes and check the ground under my feet for I felt that I must have chosen a small mound to stand upon. But there I stood on the flat earth. I felt so safe and secure. When I closed my eyes again I felt in that circle of oaks that this was the only place in all the world that was standing still and that everything else must be spinning. But when I opened my eyes again everything around me was still. I know that when the world gets too much for me to cope with, I can return here and let the world spin for awhile without me.

As I lost myself in this wonderful experience I became aware of a presence observing me. I saw a hermit like figure robed in white and he asked me to follow him. I remained where I was determined to enjoy this higher level of awareness. I was aware that he was a spirit helper rather than a tree guardian and he was very insistent that I follow him. I became aware of other visitors to the woodland and as I could see a small dog approaching, I decided it was a good time to leave the circle of oak trees. Eva and Poppy were extremely pleased as they had been getting rather exasperated with me ignoring their pleas for me to throw the ball for them. I followed the figure down a track that ran behind the oak trees. Either side of this track were evergreens of different kinds. After a short distance, he turned down a narrow track to the left which led downwards through corsican pine. I was muttering to myself about not being too happy if I ended up getting lost and was advised to stand still and absorb the energy around me.

The peace that emanated from these trees became almost tangible and I felt a little guilty for having spent the last few minutes moaning, then carried on down the track that was strewn with pine needles and suddenly the way forward was no longer clear. I started to moan again and was told to look beyond the greenery that had suddenly seemed to spring up in front of me and looking a little to the right, could again see a way through. The dogs had lost the ball and so I stood for awhile encouraging them to go back and look for it. Poppy is usually very successful at finding lost balls and soon came running back with it and we continued on our journey downwards.

After a while we came upon an even narrower track than ran left to right and I was told to go the left. The figure led the way and stopped in front of a beautiful evergreen. He told me it was a cypress and looking around me I noticed more of them together with pines and douglas fir. I had seen some cypress alongside the main path and had noticed their beautiful bark but had not been interested in working with this species. The figure in white had other ideas and told me that it was necessary to work with the energy of this tree.

Looking further on I realised that this little track joined the main path that would take us back to the car. The figure disappeared and I took out my notebook and leaned my back against the tree.

I felt a delicate pressure at the top of my head and was told that this energy can help us to link direct to the Universal Source that is within all things. I was told to strive for perfection in all that I do and to seek to make myself a channel for good. I began to feel a band of pressure around my head but it was not uncomfortable. The communication continued.

"Listen with compassion, seek and recognise justice in all you do, speak out the Truth, that all can work to release their demons of doubt and fear so that they can make progress forward upon the path of Truth. The Truth is that we are all one."

I was then told that I was not yet ready to learn any more from this species. I know that we learn only what we are ready to learn and so this was familiar to me. I still felt the peace that I had absorbed from the pine trees and now felt a deep reverence for this species of cypress. I studied the bark of the tree and noticed the rich brown and almost plum colour in places.

I picked up a small piece of branch that lay on the ground beneath the tree and marvelled at each minute green segment. So much in Nature goes un-noticed in the hurry of our busy lives. There are so many things that we hold important and necessary that are really trivial and meaningless. I thought I had learned so much in the last few years and yet I was only just beginning.

Horse Chestnut

A few days after my walk at Nutcombe Bottom, I took the dogs backup into the woodland on Dunster knoll. I wanted to see if I could find a horse chestnut to work with. There are so many different species in this wood that I felt sure that I stood a good chance of finding one. Their beauty is like that of no other species, with their lovely pink or white flowers, like wax-laden candles in the spring and their graceful leaves casting broad shadows in the sunlight.

The day was quite cool and the wind was rather strong but the dogs never seem to mind the weather, they just love to be out running around after all the different scents that come their way. We had walked one of the paths that we have walked so often passing beech, oak, yew and holly and just when I thought I was going to have to look elsewhere for a horse-chestnut, I saw one standing right next to the path. I must have passed it on so many other occasions and never looked at it properly.

There were still some of the lovely white flowers gracing its beautiful frame and its canopy cast cool shade around its base. A short distance away the trunk of an oak lay across part of the path, it looked as if it may have been struck by lightning but had held the wound until the whole of the trunk had become rotten. A scattering of petals lay upon its broken frame and I watched them rise and fall again in the wind as I linked in to the vibration of the horse chestnut.

I sensed a very balanced energy and began to see swirls of colour building up around me. A pale yellow and then a soft

Horse Chestnut

green, separate but somehow linked in harmony. The movement stopped and the forms took on almost human features which emanated such peace and acceptance of my presence. I was told that the energy of this tree species could help people to learn to balance their material and spiritual sides of life.

"We can help to keep you grounded and focused on your needs on all levels and keep your thinking in `the now` and not rushing ahead with vain possibilities. We can help you to sift through the mind`s clutter and help you to remain focused under stress. We can encourage clarity of vision when you are faced with many choices on the material level and can help you to remain balanced when making changes within your life."

The whistle from the steam train wafted up to me on the wind and brought my communication to an end. I thanked the tree for the wisdom I had been allowed to share with it but knew that I would need to return to make my own personal link in order to bring some clarity to the choices that lay ahead for me. The dogs had been sitting patiently at my feet, which surprised me, but I then remembered that I had pocketed the ball after only pretending to throw it and they must have, at last, realised this and were waiting for me to own up.

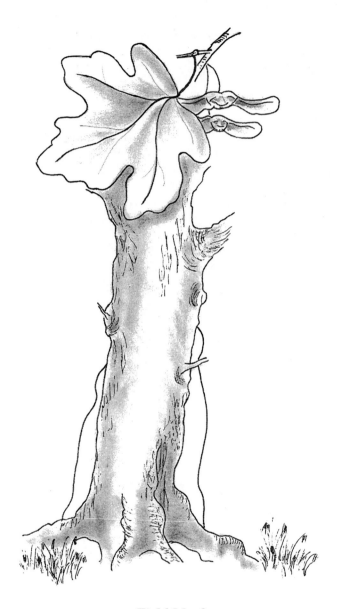

Field Maple

Field Maple

Recently walking the dogs up in the woods above the cottage, on the familiar track towards Bratton woods, I noticed a group of small trees I did not recognise. I thought at first they might be hawthorn but on closer inspection, realised that their leaves were quite a bit larger.

I looked around on the ground beneath the trees for a leaf that I could take home with me in order to check through my tree books. I didn't want to break one off deliberately and was pleased to find a new leaf lying close to the trunk one of the trees. I had walked along the path through these woods on so many occasions and had never noticed these graceful field maples as I later discovered them to be. They stand close to the path and I felt disappointed with myself for not noticing them before.

I mentally sent out my request and approached one of the taller maples and began to write as the words formed within my mind.

"We work on the heart level and teach it to sing. Where people always let their head rule over their emotions, we enable them to reach down and release themselves from that grip. Sometimes this is the result of learning to repress emotions due to a lack of nurturing during their formative years. Some people lock away their links to their emotions in order to protect themselves from past pain, which sometimes they don`t even recognise as needing to be addressed. Some protect themselves from future pain and are similarly blocked. These are people who appear to be so dependable and solid on the

outside but who cannot cope with their own emotions or those of others. They always have to be in control. Consequently, they are really only half alive. Let them come to us and free themselves, rise above the fear to experience the joy as well as the pain. In this way their full potential will be released and fulfilled. Courage is needed."

I don't know quite what I had expected from these trees but to obtain such a strong message came as a surprise. I think I still suffer from pre-conceived ideas. Perhaps I expect strong messages from tall, strong looking trees and light-hearted messages from small, delicate trees. I have so much to learn! A light, happy energy came from these wonderful trees and a strength that was both supportive and yet slightly challenging. I felt that I was being observed, almost in an effort to ensure that I understood the message correctly. When I work with spirit helpers, if I misunderstand what is being communicated to me either by my own guides or those of other people, they soon let me know. On one occasion when I took my dogs for their late evening walk, a friend's main guide came with me to explain that I had misinformed her as to the meaning of some symbols he had shown me during the development circle earlier that evening.

The next day, following his instructions, I had to telephone her to set things straight. She was quite amused at his insistence that I explain things properly. The more I work with our `unseen` supporters the more in awe I become at all the possibilities that surround us for our healing and our growth. The natural world is so much taken for granted and almost seen by many as simply a setting for a picnic but the roots of so many nations go back to a reverence for all that is around us. All of nature has a message for us, a support system that we can work with if only we can learn to listen.

Moní

Recently I had to part with my favourite cat, Moni, a beautiful nine year old Havana. I know that she is still with me but losing her physical presence has left a large gap in my life in spite of having eight other wonderful cats. She had had surgery for cancerous tumours some time before but another inoperable tumour had grown so rapidly that it took me by surprise. I felt desolate and each time I took the dogs out into the woods above the cottage, I worked with the energy of the different trees, to try to make some sense of it all and to try to loosen my grip on my sorrow. Sadness tends to draw down a barrier between this life and the next.

Together with a friend and her dog, I drove back to Nutcombe Bottom. It is so beautiful there and I had previously seen some dawn redwoods and wanted an opportunity to try to work with their energy. They have the most unusual trunks that twist and turn upwards, creating oval crevices as they grow towards the light. I mentally asked for permission to enter the aura of one of the larger specimens and leaned my head against the trunk. I didn't really expect to see or sense anything at all due to my negative state of mind. But onto my inner screen came the image of a new born baby dressed in yellow. I felt that this was a communication from one of my spirit helpers and was amazed that they had been able to get anything through to me. I felt that they were trying to tell me that she had simply moved on to a new life.

I knew this but thanked them for trying to comfort me. My greatest regret has been that I was unable to have children and I am sure that because of this I have showered the love I

would have given to my children, onto all my animals. It was therefore, quite acceptable to be shown the new baby as a symbol for new life. It was one I would understand and my helpers knew this.

I moved away from the tree and my friend and I started to walk up the wide pathway that gently rises towards the hills, our dogs racing ahead of us. I noticed that the Crown Estate had thoughtfully labelled some of the trees and also to my amusement, one of the telegraph poles, supplying it with a preservation order number too. To the left of the path stands the tallest tree in England, its height of fifty-seven metres was recorded in 1993. The trunk of this douglas fir seemed to go on for ever as it towered above us. There are more of this species along this path, each one majestic in its own right. I couldn't help but remember the one that I had chosen to work with, at the top of North Hill. It had been shaped by the wind and would never grow tall and straight like these giants. Where the path rises more sharply, we chose to turn off to the right and follow a narrow track that runs above a little stream.

Up on the slope above us were cypress and silver birch and on the other side of the stream, lambs and sheep were grazing in a field bathed in sunlight. As we threaded our way along the track we passed bluebells that were just beginning to lose their glow. Here and there were groups of pink campion, stitchwort, herb robert and foxgloves not yet in flower. And now and then we came upon a clump of one of my favourite flowers, buttercups.

After a while the path began to rise steeply up to the right but up ahead the track eventually levelled off and we found ourselves with a choice of paths. Both my friend and I were at a loss to know which path to take and so I asked my main spirit teacher. He indicated the path to the right and so we turned onto this wider path and after about ten minutes or so

I could see a familiar group of trees in the distance. We had come almost full circle and were now approaching the five large oak trees that stand on the brow of the hill above the car park.

I wanted to experience the powerful energy within this circle of trees again and walked into the centre. I couldn't feel the energy I had felt before and was disappointed but accepted that I was numb to the many energies around me. I closed my eyes and immediately saw myself about twenty years younger, I was holding my beloved cat. I couldn't stem the tears. There was a look of complete happiness on the face of this younger me as I cradled Moni. And then it was as if my tears had cleared the channels of communication between myself and these wonderful old oak trees for I began to receive a message.

"You have not lost her, she is with you always. You can now strengthen your link with her. She has much to teach you of the survival of animals."

I was then told to work with the energy of the sun to bring myself upliftment and that all I had to do was to visualise the sun itself. I left that sacred circle of oaks feeling completely different, lighter in my heart and more convinced that I could cope and move forward. My friend had been entertaining the dogs although they had now and then rushed into the circle to check on my progress. She then entered the circle to absorb the energies while I studied the piece of roughened bark that I had been told to take home with me to use as a link to the energies of the oak trees.

I have bowls of crystals at home that also hold pieces of bark, twigs or seed cases from a wide variety of trees. I sometimes sit quietly and link back to the energies and experiences that I have had with the different trees on my walks. The dogs once more excitedly ran on ahead down the path as my friend emerged from the circle of oaks. The sun was still warm and we both had gained a great deal of peace and support from those wonderful old trees.

The estuary Dunster Marsh seen from Dunster knoll

EneRgy ARound Us

Most of us have, at some time during our lives, been moved by the sight of a breathtaking sunset or sunrise, the sound of the waves moving back and forth through shingle on a beach, dew drops on the petals of a rose, the song of the sky-lark or the miracle of a child`s laughter. All of these things carry a vibration, an energy that can bring healing to us if we know how to focus upon it and absorb it.

There are everyday things around us that we can use as healing aids, colour for instance. A lot of research has been done on the therapeutic value of colour. I have learned during my work with Spirit Helpers that colour is of great interest to them.

I have been directed to teach the value of colour in our lives and the healing energy of the different colours and their respective shades. I have learned how to use it for self-healing and how to direct it for the use of distant healing. Each colour has a different energy and it can be felt and its healing quality can be experienced. Using colour within a guided meditation can tell us a great deal about where we are in our lives.

There are many thousands of people who recognise the uplifting quality of flowers and plants and spend a fortune each year on their gardens, without actually analysing why they feel uplifted when they are surrounded by such natural beauty. If asked, no doubt they would merely say that it brings them peace and a sense of tranquillity to be surrounded by such loveliness.

97

It is more than this. Everything in life emits energy and in the Natural World this energy is untainted and pure. It is this energy that we can learn to tap into in order to harness the natural healing power that exists all around us. Plants and trees can sense our energy, whether we are exhibiting stress signals or are relaxed and calm.

Quite some time ago I decided to buy a plant for my classroom and during my lunch-break I walked to the local florist. I was feeling extremely stressed due to the problems we were experiencing at school and I suppose I carried these feelings with me into the shop. As I looked at the array of beauty around me I suddenly became aware of a sense of horror emanating from the plants that I had decided to choose from. I found myself mentally promising to take the chosen plant home each evening and finally chose a pink bizzy lizzy. I took it back to the classroom and stood it in a saucer of water.

None of my pupils even noticed it on the desk in front of them. I could still feel that sense of horror from the little plant, slightly subdued but nonetheless still present and so when I arrived home that afternoon I made a promise not to take it back. It sits happily in my window, glowing and growing.

We may not be aware of it but we also give off vibrations. The different emotions that we experience emit energy that can be `read` by other people, animals and plants. During my last teaching post I had to spend at least two break-times a week monitoring the pupils at play. The school catered for boys with emotional, social and behavioural problems. Together with many other staff members, I could sense from the atmosphere around me if a fight was brewing and I would scan the playground in order to attempt to locate the source of this negative energy and deal with it before it exploded into something more serious.

Often a brief chat with the boys concerned would reduce the tension and the resulting change in the atmosphere of the play-ground was tangible. It is this often unrecognised ability to change or I would rather say, raise our vibration that is important when we wish to link in to energies of the trees.

Many thousands of people throughout the world spend time each day meditating. This act of focusing within and endeavouring to clear the mind of negative clutter from the day, effectively raises the mind's vibration enabling us to heighten our awareness of the more subtle energies within the Natural World.

Raising Your Awareness

The initial simple step of focusing on your breathing and slowing it down has a calming effect. Sometimes this is all that is needed in order to become aware of the energies around us. So if you wish to take advantage of all that is available to us within Nature first choose where you wish to walk.

Initially if you are unused to raising your vibration to enhance your awareness, you would be well-advised to leave your dogs, if you have any, at home. You need to focus and to do this, if you area beginner, walk alone. Choose a place where you will feel safe and comfortable. Obviously if you live in a city, you may not feel comfortable walking alone in the local park, so take a sympathetic friend who is not going to laugh at you as you endeavour to link in to the energies of trees.

Choose your tree, look around and approach one that you like the look of. Whether you sense anything at all, I feel that it is the right thing to do to mentally ask permission to enter the aura of the tree. All living things have an aura or energy field. Sometimes when people stand a little too close to us and it makes us feel uncomfortable we may feel that they are `taking our space`. In other words they have stepped within our auric field and this is a very sensitive area. So respect the tree. The auric field of a tree covers a large area, just remember that what you can see above the ground is mirrored by the root system beneath your feet. It may help to close your eyes, it can enable us to shut out the material world while we try to raise our awareness.

Take three deep breaths, holding each one for a few seconds and releasing them slowly, then breathe in a relaxed, gentle manner. This should help to encourage a calm state of mind where you will become more able to absorb the healing energy of the tree if this is what you wish. Simply focusing on your breathing as you stand within the energy field of a tree will enable you to absorb the healing you need.

Concentrate on what it is that is worrying you, whether it is of an emotional, spiritual or physical nature and imagine that as you breathe out you are releasing it into the atmosphere where your worries will be lifted which will enable you to deal with them more effectively. As you breathe in, imagine that you are being filled with peace and contentment. The change that will take place will be linked to your attitude regarding the particular problem.

By working with the energy of trees you will be able to release the negative state of mind that blocks your ability to see the existence of any solution. Working with the energy of trees can bring healing on many levels. All of Nature is linked to what I prefer to call, the Universal Spirit, which links all of life. We have moved so faraway from an instinctive link with the Source of life that it is difficult to believe that by linking in with the energies of trees we can tap in to that which sustains every living thing.

Trees are linked to Source naturally without the need to question. We can renew our own links with the Source or Universal Spirit by linking in to the energies of trees. Once you have begun to feel the energy around you this will give you the confidence to go further in developing your relationship with trees. If you wish to raise your awareness to a higher level in order to work at a greater depth with tree energies then I would first wish to talk to you about 'personal protection'.

As we attempt to raise our awareness even further, we place ourselves in a position of greater sensitivity. As such it then becomes important to protect our personal energy because we become more vulnerable to any negative energy that may be carried by the people around us. I have found that people who are interested in psychic or spiritual development, or those who wish to develop a relationship with the natural energies around us, are usually far more sensitive than the average person.

I have had many conversations with `sensitives` who complain of feeling drained when in the company of people who are even the slightest bit stressed or ill in any way. People who need healing for any reason, whether they are aware of it or not, simply have to stand next to a `sensitive`, in a bus queue or at a supermarket check-out, in order to absorb healing energy. Consequently, the `sensitive', may often complain about feeling drained after a simple shopping trip or after having coffee with a friend. This is because they are unaware that they are functioning naturally as a channel for healing' energy. However, if they do not know how to protect their personal energy, the healing that is drawn from them will be depleting them and making them feel very tired.

It is extremely simple to protect your personal energy. You can visualise yourself surrounded in a circle of light, you can mentally ask for circles of protection to be placed around you, addressing whatever you believe in. I have spoken to dozens of sensitives` and found that they all have their own visualisation. Basically, it is the power of thought that is at work here. If you believe that visualising yourself in a bubble of silver or gold or white light will protect your personal energy, then it will. There is nothing more powerful than the power of thought.When you have chosen your own technique for protection you can still function as a healing channel if you wish, simply by asking to be used as a channel for healing, again addressing whatever you believe in. Then when you are sitting with your friend having a cup of coffee, you will be channelling the healing energy through you not from you and you will be refreshed rather than drained.

Working with the different vibrations of trees at a deeper level again requires you to protect your personal energy. Working at this level your awareness is raised to a more sensitive pitch and protecting yourself allows you to experience these powerful energies without feeling drained.

After you have focused on your breathing in order to slow it down and then used your own personal protection technique, you can then focus your attention on opening up your energy centres or Chakras. This raises your awareness further. There have been so many books written on Chakras. My teaching guides have encouraged me to teach people to put aside the colours associated with each energy centre and have told me to instead enable people to simply focus on each Chakra in turn, starting with the base and allowing a colour or a sensation to build up. Some people feel rather than see. You eventually learn to interpret the colours or sensations that you become aware of at each centre and this enables you to understand and monitor your physical, emotional and spiritual progress.

For instance, when I take a look at my own energy centres I see a mucky browny-orange at my sacral chakra. I had major abdominal surgery over a year ago and my recovery has been very slow. Being able to check my progress in this area has been a comforting and educational process. Equally when I check on my heart centre, I usually see pink. It is more important to assess exactly how I feel about pink than to rush and consult one of the multitude of books that exist on this subject. For me, pink tells me that I am still in need of some self-nurturing. It may mean something entirely different to someone else, but what is important, is what I feel it means to me.

When you have opened up your energy centres you will have raised your ability to sense the energies of the trees. People sense these energies in many different ways. You may initially feel a tingling in your fingers, hands and sometimes even your feet. You may experience a cold or even a hot feeling. You may begin to receive telepathic communication, feeling almost compelled to write what you are receiving. So many people who follow the path of spiritual or psychic development experience tremendous doubts about what they sense, see or hear, telepathically or otherwise.

Try to put your doubts aside, open your mind and keep a note of all you experience. If you feel a profound sense of peace, note the species of tree that you are working with. If you sense negativity from a tree or feel negative towards a particular tree, note it down. Sit down with your back to the tree and work through the feeling.

Examine your own fears and your doubts, locate the problem and don't shy away from what the tree is trying to show you. The sensation you experience may be a mirroring of what you carry within you. Breathe slowly and deeply and release the fear and the negative sensation will lift as you link in to the healing potential of the tree. If you experience something too challenging as I did when I first worked with the energy of a beech tree, move away, but don't, as I did, avoid working with the species.

Examine why you are sensing this challenging energy. Is there something in your life that needs addressing? Work with the energy of a different species and then return to the one that challenged you. Note any change in the energy that you sense. It will enable you to see whether you have moved on with your problem or if you need to work harder with it. Above all - be kind to yourself. We are all on a long journey of learning.

There is so much around us that can give us the nurturing that we need in order to take another step forward on our path. I don`t think that I have met anyone who does not have some problem or other that is holding them back or clouding their vision. If only we could stand for a while and just look around at all that exists within Nature that we sadly take for granted. If we could just take the time to look closely at the petals of a flower, or allow ourselves to really feel the breeze upon our face or lean our back against the trunk of an old oak tree in the hush of twilight. Make time for yourself, for your healing, for your growth. For as you clear your past of any pain or sorrow that has held you back, you will clear a path for healing to work through you to benefit others around you. Accept that you deserve to be made whole again and learn that there exists all around you in Nature the healing energy to take you forward.

A Tree Meditation

Sometimes it may be difficult for you to leave your home in order to benefit from the peace and tranquillity that you can gain from linking in with tree energies. At such a time you can use the following meditation to bring you closer to the harmony that you need.

Make sure that you are sitting in a comfortable chair and that you have done your chosen form of protection and have also opened up your energy centres. It is important not to be disturbed during the meditation as it can cause quite a jolt to be brought out of a tranquil and peaceful state to one of noise.

If you wish you can ask a friend or partner to gently and quietly call your name after a chosen length of time. Twenty minutes is usually sufficient for the type of meditation that I work with. You may choose to put the meditation onto a tape but it can be difficult to block out the background hum that usually surfaces when I try to tape anything. I asked my spirit teachers to give me an appropriate meditation for you and so I do hope you enjoy it -

You find yourself in a comfortable chair, a strip of carpet laid out before you leading to three steps that take you upwards into a lit corridor. You feel safe, you feel secure, you are in complete control. You walk out of the door at the end of the corridor which takes you into a beautiful garden. The sun is high in the sky and you can feel its gentle warmth on your skin. You can also feel a soft breeze as it blows gently around you. You follow the path as it leads past flowers in full bloom until you come to the garden gate. You open the gate and walk out of the garden onto a narrow lane. The lane is bordered by a hedge on one side and by beautiful young trees on the other. You can hear bird-song around you and you look up into the branches of one of the trees and watch for awhile a little bird that is singing to you.You walk on a little further and you notice that the lane is leading to a sunlit glade. You stand quite still just absorbing the peace of this place and then as you look around at the trees that grace the fringe of the glade, you notice a large tree, the lower branches almost touching the ground. It is one of your favourite trees and as you approach it you mentally ask to step within its aura. You are greeted with a welcoming and supporting energy and decide to sit on the ground and rest your back against the trunk of this beautiful tree.

You begin to feel a wonderful sense of peace as you breathe in the healing energy of this tree.You feel totally at peace with yourself and all around you. When you feel ready to return to the garden, you stand and thank the tree for its healing energy and turn back towards the lane. You can still feel the gentle warmth of the sun and are wrapped in the peace that was freely given to you by that wonderful tree. After a while you reach the garden gate and walking through it, walk along the path, once again passing the beautiful flowers that grace every corner. Then once more you enter the lit corridor and walk back towards the three steps that will take you down onto the little strip of carpet and back to your comfortable chair. When you are ready, open your eyes. Having a glass of water ready for you to drink from will help you to come back to your usual vibration, but you must remember to close down your energy centres before you leave your chair. otherwise if you were then to find yourself in the company of someone who is unwell, on any level, you could absorb their symptoms. However, if you are very experienced, I find that simply protecting my personal energy allows me to keep my energy centres open without any harmful effect. But I do not recommend this for anyone who is not in full control of their sensing ability. I do not close down my energy centres because I am always chatting to spirit guides or friends but I always protect myself. It sounds as if this is all similar to a dangerous sport - it isn't but wherever you find yourself you may experience negative and positive energy, I mean from the living, and you need to be aware of how to protect yourself it you are sensitive to those energies. From my experience, it is a wonderful way to live. I work each day to become more in tune with all that is around me. I know that I have a long way to go but I also know that there is so much around me to guide, heal and support me along my way. I wish you great joy in this wonderful adventure.

If you wish to contact the author regarding workshops, courses, meditation tapes on Psychic and Spiritual development, or working with Earth Energies you can write to: Primrose Cottage, 11, Woodcombe Cottages, Minehead, Somerset, TA24 8SE

Magical Guardians - Exploring the Spirit and Nature of Trees
by Philip Heselton

"straightforward, unpretentious account of how to build up a personal relationship with your favourite tree - memorable pictures" (3RD Stone) *"deals with trees as wise and sentient beings we can communicate with by contacting their inner energy...Highly recommended"* The Cauldron This is a book about trees, but a book with a difference, for it acknowledges trees to be wise beings who can teach us much if we approach them in the right way. This book shows how to go about it, revealing the origins of our awakening interest in - and love for - trees. Trees have a spiritual nature, and opening up to this spirit has been a constant feature in human society. Through practical guidance, this book gives hints on how we can make that contact for ourselves. The personalities of the ancient trees - our Magical Guardians - are explored, and the book reveals how we can start to acquire some of their deeper meanings. ISBN 1 86163 057 3   £11.95

The Enchanted Forest - The Magical Lore of Trees by Yvonne Aburrow
"..wonderful insight...easy to read...very informative, a lovely enchanting book". *Touchstone (OBOD)* Fascinating & truly unique - a comprehensive guide to the magical, medicinal & craft uses, mythology, folklore, symbolism & weatherlore of trees. There are chapters on trees in myth & legend, tree spirits, trees in ritual magic, trees & alphabets (runes & Ogham) & weather lore. These chapters are followed by a comprehensive 'herbal index' with in-depth coverage of individual trees from acacia to aspen, wayfaring tree to willow. Profusely illustrated. ISBN 1898307 083   £10.95

Tree: Essence, Spirit and Teacher   by Simon & Sue Lilly
Trees are the creators and maintainers of our reality. In every tradition their spiritual strength has been clearly recognised. Sue and Simon Lilly, developers of *"Green Man Tree Essences"*, share their experiences and describe a wide range of techniques by which we can come into a direct and powerful relationship with the Tree Kingdoms. Emphasis is placed on establishing a personal experience through which the teachings of the Tree Spirits can become apparent. Subjects covered include: The metaphysical reality of trees, Tree essences and how to use them; Meeting the Spirits - methods of communication; Tree Teacher Techniques; Attunements to forty different trees; Coming into the presence of tree energies through initiation, and an exploration of some powerful Tree Teachers. This is the first volume in the *"Tree Seer"* series. ISBN 18163 084 0   £15.95

The Sacred Grove - The Mysteries of the Forest by Yvonne Aburrow
"Such a journey through sometimes tangled and conflicting opinions is delightfully possible with this excellent anthology which pulsates with life and creates an immediate response for the reader. Almost anything anyone would need to know about tree worship is contained in this volume...a modern classic. It is quite true that I gained and learned more in a day or two from reading this book than I have from similar reading over many years. This is a tribute to the author who illuminates where others have tended to obscure. I shall certainly return to this book on many future occasions for sheer pleasure as well as for more information." *Prediction* magazine ISBN   1898307 12 1   £10.95

FREE DETAILED CATALOGUE

Capall Bann is owned and run by people actively involved in many of the areas in which we publish. A detailed illustrated catalogue is available on request, SAE or International Postal Coupon appreciated. **Titles can be ordered direct from Capall Bann, post free in the UK** (cheque or PO with order) or from good bookshops and specialist outlets.

Do contact us for details on the latest releases at: **Capall Bann Publishing, Freshfields, Chieveley, Berks, RG20 8TF.** Titles include:

Angels and Goddesses - Celtic Christianity & Paganism, M. Howard
Arthur - The Legend Unveiled, C Johnson & E Lung
Auguries and Omens - The Magical Lore of Birds, Yvonne Aburrow
Asyniur - Womens Mysteries in the Northern Tradition, S McGrath
Beginnings - Geomancy, Builder's Rites & Electional Astrology in the
    European Tradition, Nigel Pennick
Between Earth and Sky, Julia Day
Caer Sidhe - Celtic Astrology and Astronomy, Michael Bayley
Call of the Horned Piper, Nigel Jackson
Cat's Company, Ann Walker
Celtic Faery Shamanism, Catrin James
Celtic Faery Shamanism - The Wisdom of the Otherworld, Catrin James
Celtic Lore & Druidic Ritual, Rhiannon Ryall
Celtic Sacrifice - Pre Christian Ritual & Religion, Marion Pearce
Celtic Saints and the Glastonbury Zodiac, Mary Caine
Creating Form From the Mist - The Wisdom of Women in Celtic Myth and
    Culture, Lynne Sinclair-Wood
Crystal Clear - A Guide to Quartz Crystal, Jennifer Dent
Crystal Doorways, Simon & Sue Lilly
Crossing the Borderlines - Guising, Masking & Ritual Animal Disguise in the
    European Tradition, Nigel Pennick
Dragons of the West, Nigel Pennick
Earth Dance - A Year of Pagan Rituals, Jan Brodie
Earth Harmony - Places of Power, Holiness & Healing, Nigel Pennick
Earth Magic, Margaret McArthur
Eildon Tree (The) Romany Language & Lore, Michael Hoadley
Enchanted Forest - The Magical Lore of Trees, Yvonne Aburrow
Eternal Priestess, Sage Weston
Eternally Yours Faithfully, Roy Radford & Evelyn Gregory
Everything You Always Wanted To Know About Your Body, But So Far
    Nobody's Been Able To Tell You, Chris Thomas & D Baker

Face of the Deep - Healing Body & Soul, Penny Allen
Fairies in the Irish Tradition, Molly Gowen
Familiars - Animal Powers of Britain, Anna Franklin
Forest Paths - Tree Divination, Brian Harrison, Ill. S. Rouse
From Past to Future Life, Dr Roger Webber
Gardening For Wildlife Ron Wilson
God Year, The, Nigel Pennick & Helen Field
Goddess Year, The, Nigel Pennick & Helen Field
Goddesses, Guardians & Groves, Jack Gale
Handbook For Pagan Healers, Liz Joan
Handbook of Fairies, Ronan Coghlan
Healing Book, The, Chris Thomas and Diane Baker
Healing Homes, Jennifer Dent
Healing Journeys, Paul Williamson
Healing Stones, Sue Philips
Herb Craft - Shamanic & Ritual Use of Herbs, Lavender & Franklin
In Search of Herne the Hunter, Eric Fitch
Inner Celtia, Alan Richardson & David Annwn
Inner Mysteries of the Goths, Nigel Pennick
Inner Space Workbook - Develop Thru Tarot, C Summers & J Vayne
Intuitive Journey, Ann Walker Isis - African Queen, Akkadia Ford
Journey Home, The, Chris Thomas
Kecks, Keddles & Kesh - Celtic Lang & The Cog Almanac, Bayley
Language of the Psycards, Berenice
Legend of Robin Hood, The, Richard Rutherford-Moore
Lid Off the Cauldron, Patricia Crowther
Light From the Shadows - Modern Traditional Witchcraft, Gwyn
Lore of the Sacred Horse, Marion Davies
Magic of Herbs - A Complete Home Herbal, Rhiannon Ryall
Magical Guardians - Exploring the Spirit and Nature of Trees, Philip Heselton
Magical History of the Horse, Janet Farrar & Virginia Russell
Magical Lore of Animals, Yvonne Aburrow
Magical Lore of Cats, Marion Davies
Magical Lore of Herbs, Marion Davies
Magick Without Peers, Ariadne Rainbird & David Rankine
Mind Massage - 60 Creative Visualisations, Marlene Maundrill
Mirrors of Magic - Evoking the Spirit of the Dewponds, P Heselton
Moon Mysteries, Jan Brodie
Mysteries of the Runes, Michael Howard
Mystic Life of Animals, Ann Walker
Pagan Feasts - Seasonal Food for the 8 Festivals, Franklin & Phillips
Patchwork of Magic - Living in a Pagan World, Julia Day
Pathworking - A Practical Book of Guided Meditations, Pete Jennings
Pillars of Tubal Cain, Nigel Jackson
Places of Pilgrimage and Healing, Adrian Cooper
Practical Divining, Richard Foord

Practical Meditation, Steve Hounsome
Practical Spirituality, Steve Hounsome
Psychic Self Defence - Real Solutions, Jan Brodie
Real Fairies, David Tame
Reality - How It Works & Why It Mostly Doesn't, Rik Dent
Romany Tapestry, Michael Houghton
Sacred Animals, Gordon MacLellan
Sacred Celtic Animals, Marion Davies, Ill. Simon Rouse
Sacred Dorset - On the Path of the Dragon, Peter Knight
Sacred Grove - The Mysteries of the Forest, Yvonne Aburrow
Sacred Geometry, Nigel Pennick
Sacred Nature, Ancient Wisdom & Modern Meanings, A Cooper
Sacred Ring - Pagan Origins of British Folk Festivals, M. Howard
Season of Sorcery - On Becoming a Wisewoman, Poppy Palin
Seasonal Magic - Diary of a Village Witch, Paddy Slade
Secret Places of the Goddess, Philip Heselton
Secret Signs & Sigils, Nigel Pennick
Self Enlightenment, Mayan O'Brien
Spirits of the Earth series, Jaq D Hawkins
Stony Gaze, Investigating Celtic Heads John Billingsley
Talking to the Earth, Gordon MacLellan
Teachings of the Wisewomen, Rhiannon Ryall
The Other Kingdoms Speak, Helena Hawley
Tree: Essence of Healing, Simon & Sue Lilly
Tree: Essence, Spirit & Teacher, Simon & Sue Lilly
Understanding Chaos Magic, Jaq D Hawkins
Warp and Weft - In Search of the I-Ching, William de Fancourt
Warriors at the Edge of Time, Jan Fry
Water Witches, Tony Steele
West Country Wicca, Rhiannon Ryall
Wildwitch - The Craft of the Natural Psychic, Poppy Palin
Wildwood King , Philip Kane
Wondrous Land - The Faery Faith of Ireland by Dr Kay Mullin
Working With the Merlin, Geoff Hughes
Your Talking Pet, Ann Walker

FREE detailed catalogue and FREE 'Inspiration' magazine

Contact: Capall Bann Publishing, Freshfields, Chieveley, Berks, RG20 8TF

Capall Bann has moved from Berkshire and is now at:

Auton Farm
Milverton
Somerset
TA4 1NE

Tel 01823 401528
www.capallbann.co.uk
enquiries@capallbann.co.uk

A full detailed catalogue is available on request

Capall Bann has moved
from Berkshire and is now
at:

Auton Farm
Milverton
Somerset
TA4 1NE

Tel 01823 401528
www.capallbann.co.uk
enquiries@capallbann.co.uk

A full detailed catalogue is
available on request